W9-BUQ-407

WORLD WAR II
WEAPONS

BY JOHN HAMILTON

VISIT US AT
WWW.ABDOPUBLISHING.COM

Published by ABDO Publishing Company, 8000 West 78th Street, Suite 310, Edina, MN 55439. Copyright ©2012 by Abdo Consulting Group, Inc. International copyrights reserved in all countries. No part of this book may be reproduced in any form without written permission from the publisher. ABDO & Daughters™ is a trademark and logo of ABDO Publishing Company.

Printed in the United States of America, North Mankato, Minnesota.
052011
092011

Editor: Sue Hamilton
Graphic Design: John Hamilton
Cover Design: Neil Klinepier
Cover Photo: National Archives and Records Administration (NARA)
Interior Photos and Illustrations: Alexpl, p. 20; Anynobody, p. 20; AP Images, p. 16; Curiousandrelics, p. 8 ; Getty Images, p. 8, 9, 11, 13, 16, 17, 20, 24, 25, 27, 29; John Hamilton, p. 22-23; NARA, p. 4-5, 6-7, 10, 11, 12-13, 13, 14-15, 18-19, 21, 26-27, 28; Igor Kurtukov, p. 16; Grzegorz Pietrzak, p. 9; iStockphoto, p. 10; Oberiko, p. 9; Mark Pellegrini, p. 16; Phanatic, p. 8; George Shuklin, p. 9.

ABDO Booklinks
To learn more about World War II, visit ABDO Publishing Company online. Web sites about World War II are featured on our Book Links pages. These links are routinely monitored and updated to provide the most current information available. Website: www.abdopublishing.com

Library of Congress Cataloging-in-Publication Data

Hamilton, John, 1959-
  World War II. Weapons / John Hamilton.
    p. cm. -- (World War II)
  Includes index.
  ISBN 978-1-61783-064-8
  1. Military weapons--History--20th century--Juvenile literature. 2. World War, 1939-1945--Equipment and supplies--Juvenile literature. I. Title. II. Title: Weapons.
  UF500.H354 2012
  623.409'044--dc22
                        2011015970

CONTENTS

THE WEAPONS OF WWII

World War II was fought between 1939-1945. It was the largest war in history. All of the world's major powers participated, including the United States, Great Britain, the Soviet Union, Germany, Japan, Italy, France, China, Canada, and Australia.

When the war began in 1939, many of the weapons used were not very modern. Some countries were still using horse cavalry and biplanes! Nazi Germany and Japan had superior weapons at first. Germany defeated Poland in about a month using powerful tanks and dive bombers.

In just a few short years, the major powers used their industrial strength and scientific knowledge to create new weapons at a rapid pace. These modernized tools of destruction were produced in mass quantities, more than in any time in history.

World War II began a new trend in how wars are won or lost. Leadership, battlefield tactics, and troop morale remain important. But beginning with World War II, the side that produces the most technologically advanced weapons, in mass quantities, has a huge advantage in winning the long, deadly tragedy of modern warfare.

Massive 16-inch (41-cm) guns on the United States battleship USS *Iowa* bombard enemy targets in the Pacific Ocean during the war against Japan.

INFANTRY WEAPONS

A U.S. Marine draws a bead on a Japanese sniper on the island of Okinawa during the Pacific campaign against Japan. He is shooting a Thompson M1928 .45-caliber submachine gun. It weighed 10.7 pounds (4.9 kg). It had a firing rate of 675 rounds per minute, with a normal range of about 160 feet (49 m).

Many of the weapons used by individual soldiers in World War II were not much different than those used in World War I (1914–1918). Long-range rifles that worked well on the open battlefields of the Great War worked just as well during World War II.

However, World War II also included new kinds of fighting in urban areas and thick jungles. From the shattered streets of Stalingrad, Russia, to the tropical rain forests of Guadalcanal, speed and mobility became very important to winning battles.

Factories invented new ways of riveting and welding that produced mass quantities of reliable and deadly firearms. "Automatic" weapons could reload themselves rapidly after each shot. These machine guns weren't as accurate as rifles, but they didn't need to be. A single soldier armed with a machine gun could wipe out an entire enemy squad at close range.

Personal weapons included more than firearms. Hand grenades, flamethrowers, and anti-tank weapons such as bazookas turned World War II battlefields into dangerous killing grounds.

United States

M1 Garand Rifle

Caliber:	0.3 in.
Firing rate:	30 rounds per minute
Magazine capacity:	8 rounds
Weight:	9.6 pounds (4.4 kg)
Range:	656 yards (600 m)

Notes: The first semi-automatic rifle in military service, the M1 Garand gave U.S. ground troops much-needed firepower. It was heavy but stable, with low recoil for accurate shots.

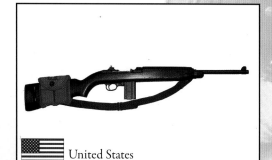

United States

M1 Carbine

Caliber:	0.3 in.
Firing rate:	45 rounds per minute
Magazine capacity:	8 rounds
Weight:	5.2 pounds (2.4 kg)
Range:	273 yards (250 m)

Notes: The M1 Carbine was lighter than the Garand, with a better firing rate. It was used mainly by officers, paratroopers, and soldiers who hauled heavy loads, such as mortar teams.

Germany

MG 42 Machine Gun

Caliber:	0.3 in.
Firing rate:	1,500 rounds per minute
Magazine capacity:	50 or 250 rounds
Weight:	25.5 pounds (11.6 kg)
Range:	1,312 yards (1,200 m)

Notes: The German MG 42 was considered by many to be the best machine gun of the war. It had a very high rate of fire, was simple to manufacture, and worked even in cold or muddy conditions.

United States

Browning Automatic Rifle (BAR)

Caliber:	0.3 in.
Firing rate:	350 to 550 rounds per minute
Magazine capacity:	20 rounds
Weight:	20.9 pounds (9.5 kg)
Range:	875 yards (800 m)

Notes: The BAR was a light machine gun, but because of its small magazine that held only 20 rounds, it worked best with short bursts instead of continuous fire.

Sten Machine Pistol

Caliber:	0.35 in.
Firing rate:	500 rounds per minute
Magazine capacity:	32 rounds
Weight:	6.6 pounds (3 kg)
Range:	219 yards (200 m)

Notes: This effective British machine pistol was simple and cheap to manufacture. Its name comes from its two designers: R.V. Shepperd and H.J. Turpin, who worked at the Enfield gun factory.

United Kingdom

Shpagin PPSh-41 Machine Pistol

Caliber:	0.3 in.
Firing rate:	900 rounds per minute
Magazine capacity:	71 rounds
Weight:	11.6 pounds (5.3 kg)
Range:	219 yards (200 m)

Notes: This Soviet machine pistol was first used by the Red Army in 1940. It was accurate, reliable, and performed well even under extreme combat conditions. A disadvantage was its weight.

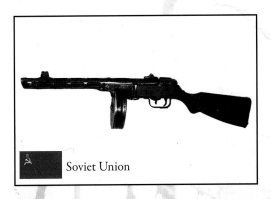
Soviet Union

MP 40 Machine Pistol

Caliber:	0.35 in.
Firing rate:	400 rounds per minute
Magazine capacity:	32 rounds
Weight:	7.9 pounds (3.6 kg)
Range:	219 yards (200 m)

Notes: The MP 40 machine pistol, along with the earlier design, the MP 38, was designed for close combat, such as in cities and buildings. It was accurate, but jammed if mishandled.

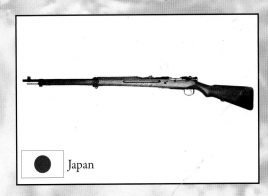
Germany

Arisaka Type 99 Rifle

Caliber:	0.3 in.
Magazine capacity:	5 rounds
Weight:	8.4 pounds (3.8 kg)
Range:	656 yards (600 m)

Notes: The Arisaka Type 99 was a bolt-action rifle used by the Japanese Imperial Army. After firing, the soldier reloaded by turning a bolt that opened the breach, the rear of the barrel. The Type 99 was similar to the German Mauser 98k rifle.

Japan

Germany

Luger P08 Pistol

Caliber:	0.35 in.
Magazine capacity:	8 rounds
Weight:	2.1 pounds (1 kg)
Range:	55 yards (50 m)

Notes: The Luger P08 was introduced as a standard handgun of the German army in 1908. It was used in both World War I and World War II. The P08 was reliable and accurate, but expensive to make. It was replaced by the similar Walther P38 in 1942.

United States

Colt M 1911 Pistol

Caliber:	0.45 in.
Magazine capacity:	7 rounds
Weight:	2.4 pounds (1 kg)
Range:	55 yards (50 m)

Notes: Considered one of the best pistols ever made, the Colt M 1911 was a standard sidearm of U.S. Army soldiers in World War II and for years afterwards. It was very reliable, and its large-caliber bullet had tremendous stopping power.

United Kingdom

Bren Light Machine Gun

Caliber:	0.303 in.
Firing rate:	500 rounds per minute
Magazine capacity:	30 rounds
Weight:	22.5 pounds (10.2 kg)
Range:	711 yards (650 m)

Notes: The Bren was a standard light machine gun used by British forces. Usually reliable, it could sometimes jam because of its .303-caliber ammunition.

United States

Browning M2 Heavy Machine Gun

Caliber:	0.5 in.
Firing rate:	500 rounds per minute
Magazine capacity:	110 rounds
Weight:	84 pounds (38 kg)
Range:	2,187 yards (2,000 m)

Notes: The M2 was intended to defend armored vehicles and aircraft. It was also used on ships. Its .50-caliber ammunition could penetrate armor more than 500 yards (457 m) away.

Flamethrower 35

Weight:	79 pounds (35.8 kg)
Flammable liquid capacity:	3.1 gallons (11.7 liter)
Bursts:	2 to 15
Range:	27 to 33 yards (25 to 30 m)

Notes: Flamethrowers were used by the Allies and Axis during World War II to clear bunkers and armored vehicles. The Flamethrower 35 was Germany's first model. It was heavy and extremely dangerous to use.

Germany

Bazooka M1

Caliber:	2.3 in.
Length:	54.7 inches (139 cm)
Weight:	12.7 pounds (5.8 kg)
Range:	219 yards (200 m)

Notes: The Bazooka was an American anti-tank weapon. It was basically a metal tube open at both ends. A small rocket was inserted in the back and electrically ignited, with little recoil. Individual soldiers could defend against tanks at a distance.

United States

Model 24 Hand Grenade

Length:	14 inches (36 cm)
Weight:	1 pound, 11 ounces (.8 kg)
Range:	30 to 40 yards (27 to 37 m)
Blast Radius:	12 to 14 yards (11 to 13 m)

Notes: The German Model 24 was also known as a potato masher, or stick grenade. It had a steel head with an explosive filler, and a wooden handle. The handle gave the soldier leverage, which meant it had a longer throwing distance than other grenades.

Germany

M1 81mm Mortar

Caliber:	3.2 in.
Barrel Length:	45.6 inches (115.8 cm)
Weight:	136 pounds (61.7 kg)
Range:	3,292 yards (3,010 m)

Notes: The American M1 mortar was a smooth-bore weapon that fired explosive shells at a high angle, allowing troops to fire into trenches or over low obstacles. Shells with stabilizer fins were loaded from the front muzzle.

United States

ARTILLERY
AND MISSILES

Artillery pieces are large cannons used in warfare. They came in many shapes and sizes during World War II. They were used to rain down explosives on the enemy from long distances.

Artillery ranged from portable pieces such as mortars to gigantic cannons that traveled by railway. For the most part, artillery pieces had wheels and were hauled by trucks or tractors.

The projectiles fired by artillery are called shells. Most were filled with explosives to attack enemy troops. Some were designed to destroy tanks or aircraft. Others produced smoke, hiding the movement of attacking ground troops and vehicles. Mortars and howitzers, which lob shells in a high arc, were especially effective in rugged mountain areas.

Germany used unmanned missiles, including slow-moving V-1 "buzz bombs," and V-2 rockets that could fly 3,400 miles per hour (5,472 kph). Fortunately for the Allies, they were not very accurate.

American soldiers pose on the barrel of a captured German 274mm rail cannon. These mammoth artillery weapons had a range of over 70 miles (113 km), but were difficult to fire accurately and very expensive to manufacture and operate.

American soldiers fire an M2A1 105mm howitzer at German forces in France in 1944.

German V-2 rockets were deadly but inaccurate. Each carried 2,148 pounds (974 kg) of explosives.

TANKS

During the invasion of France in 1940, Germany proved how effective tanks could be. Tanks are heavy military vehicles that drive on tracks, which helps them move over rough ground without becoming easily stuck. They are armed with a large cannon and smaller machine gun, and have thick armor to protect the crew inside.

During the first part of World War II, Germany had superior tanks, such as the Panzer IV. Eventually, the Allies developed good tanks of their own, such as the Sherman tank from the United States, and the T-34 from the Soviet Union. Sherman tanks weren't as formidable as German Panther or Tiger tanks, but they were reliable, and there were more of them.

The German *blitzkrieg* (lightning warfare) was a battle tactic that used "combined arms." Tanks were very effective when combined with foot soldiers (mobile infantry) and aircraft.

Battles were no longer won by both sides slugging it out in trenches or fixed positions, like in World War I. Instead, the fighting forces of World War II swept across the landscape with speed and coordination.

Mobility, firepower, and the ability to adapt to changing conditions determined the victor, and tanks played a major role.

A squad of American soldiers uses a Sherman tank as cover while patrolling a town in Belgium in 1944.

Germany

Panzer IV

Weight:	28 tons (25 metric tons)
Maximum Speed:	24 miles per hour (39 kph)
Armor:	0.4–3.1 inches (1–7.9 cm)
Main Armament:	3-inch (7.6-cm) cannon
Crew:	5

Notes: Germany relied on the Panzer IV throughout the war. It was a solid workhorse, with thick armor and a powerful cannon. Metal skirts on the sides protected it against anti-tank explosives.

Germany

Panzer V (Panther)

Weight:	50 tons (45 metric tons)
Maximum Speed:	29 miles per hour (47 kph)
Armor:	1–3.8 inches (2.5–9.7 cm)
Main Armament:	3-inch (7.6-cm) cannon
Crew:	5

Notes: The Panther was built to counter the Soviet T-34 tank. It had thick armor that was angled to deflect enemy fire. It was highly maneuverable, and was one of the best tanks of the war.

Germany

Panzer VI (Tiger)

Weight:	60 tons (54 metric tons)
Maximum Speed:	24 miles per hour (39 kph)
Armor:	1–4.3 inches (2.5–10.9 cm)
Main Armament:	3.5-inch (8.8-cm) cannon
Crew:	5

Notes: The legendary Tiger tank was very heavy because of its thick armor. It withstood most attacks, and its powerful cannon could penetrate almost any enemy armored vehicle.

Japan

Type 95 Ha-Go

Weight:	8 tons (7 metric tons)
Maximum Speed:	28 miles per hour (45 kph)
Armor:	0.23–0.5 inches (0.58–1.3 cm)
Main Armament:	1.5-inch (3.8-cm) cannon
Crew:	3

Notes: Small, lightweight, and with relatively thin armor, the Japanese Type 95 Ha-Go was used mainly to support ground troops. It was reliable, but easily destroyed by anti-tank weapons.

Valentine Mk. 1

Weight:	18 tons (16 metric tons)
Maximum Speed:	15 miles per hour (24 kph)
Armor:	0.3–2.6 inches (0.8–6.6 cm)
Main Armament:	2-pndr 1.6-in (4 cm) cannon
Crew:	3

Notes: The British Valentine Mk. 1 had a reliable engine and thick armor, but it was slow. It also had a weak cannon. Nevertheless, it was manufactured in great quantities during the war.

United Kingdom

T-34

Weight:	35 tons (32 metric tons)
Maximum Speed:	31 miles per hour (50 kph)
Armor:	0.9–3.5 inches (2.3–8.9 cm)
Main Armament:	3.3-inch (8.4-cm) cannon
Crew:	5

Notes: Considered by many to be the best overall tank of World War II, the Soviet T-34 combined firepower, mobility, and thick, sloping armor, which deflected enemy fire.

Soviet Union

M4 Sherman

Weight:	35 tons(32 metric tons)
Maximum Speed:	25 miles per hour (40 kph)
Armor:	0.5–4.1 inches (1.3–10.4 cm)
Main Armament:	3-inch (7.6 cm) cannon
Crew:	5

Notes: The M4 Sherman was the main American tank of World War II. It was mechanically reliable, had thick armor, a powerful stabilized cannon, and was produced in great numbers.

United States

M26 Pershing

Weight:	46 tons (42 metric tons)
Maximum Speed:	25 miles per hour (40 kph)
Armor:	0.5–4.5 inches (1.3–11.4 cm)
Main Armament:	3.5-inch (9 cm) cannon
Crew:	5

Notes: The heavy, powerful U.S. M26 Pershing tank was developed to counter the threat from Germany's Panther and Tiger tanks. It entered service toward the end of the war in 1945.

United States

SHIPS

Controlling the seas was critical in moving troops and supplies during World War II. "Commerce raiding" involved sinking the other side's cargo ships. It was very effective at choking off supplies.

Germany used a fleet of more than 1,000 deep-diving submarines called *U-boats* to terrorize the Atlantic Ocean, sinking almost 3,000 Allied ships.

The Allies responded with submarines of their own, plus convoys and regular patrols that used newly developed sonar and depth charges. In the Pacific Ocean, the Imperial Navy of Japan was crippled by American submarines.

Massive battleships, deadly cruisers, and swift destroyers all played a role in World War II, including commerce raiding, blockading ports, and bombarding enemy shore positions. But it was aircraft carriers that changed the face of naval warfare. These large "flattops," with decks longer than a football field, sent waves of dive bombers to attack far-flung targets. Regular surface ships became sitting ducks.

Aircraft carriers were responsible for the American victories over Japan in the Battle of the Coral Sea and the Battle of Midway in 1942. The Battle of Midway, especially, put Japan on the defensive for the rest of the war, and yet neither fleet saw each other during the course of the battle. Air power had become a crucial part of victory at sea.

The American aircraft carrier USS *Langley* leads a carrier task force back to anchorage after striking targets in the Philippines in the Pacific Ocean in 1944.

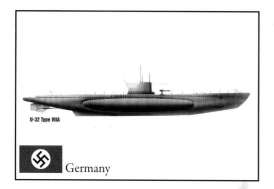

Germany

U-boat Type VIIC (submarine)

Length:	220 feet (67 m)
Maximum Speed:	18 knots (21 mph/33 kph)
Range (surfaced):	9,782 miles (15,743 km)
Diving Depth:	330 feet (101 m)
Torpedoes:	14
Crew:	44

Notes: The workhorse of Germany's submarine fleet, the U-boat Type VII was very maneuverable, had a long range, and a powerful striking ability.

Germany

Bismarck (battleship)

Length:	821 feet (250 m)
Displacement:	45,590 tons
Maximum Speed:	30 knots (35 mph/56 kph)
Range:	9,321 miles (15,001 km)
Crew:	2,200

Notes: The *Bismarck* and its sister ship, the *Tirpitz*, were the largest ships built by the German navy. In 1941, the *Bismarck* sank the British battlecruiser HMS *Hood*. The British later sank the *Bismarck*.

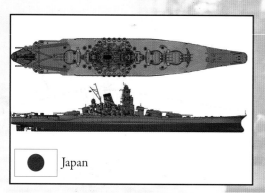

Japan

Yamato (battleship)

Length:	864 feet (263 m)
Displacement:	69,646 tons
Maximum Speed:	28 knots (32 mph/52 kph)
Range:	8,631 miles (13,890 km)
Crew:	44

Notes: The *Yamato*-class battleship from Japan was the largest and most heavily armed ship in the world. On April 7, 1945, the *Yamato* was sunk by dozens of American aircraft carrier-based planes.

United Kingdom

HMS *Prince of Wales* (battleship)

Length:	745 feet (227 m)
Displacement:	38,000 tons
Maximum Speed:	28 knots (32 mph/52 kph)
Range:	16,686 miles (26,854 km)
Crew:	1,521

Notes: The HMS *Prince of Wales* was a *King George V*-class battleship, the most advanced British design of the war. It fought against the *Bismarck*. Japanese planes sank it on December 10, 1941.

USS *Missouri* (battleship)

Length:	887 feet (270 m)
Displacement:	48,500 tons
Maximum Speed:	33 knots (38 mph/61 kph)
Range:	19,103 miles (30,743 km)
Crew:	2,800

Notes: The USS *Missouri* was an *Iowa*-class ship, the largest and most powerful battleships built by the United States. The *Missouri* was fast, had thick armor, and massive 16-inch (41 cm) guns.

United States

Kaga (aircraft carrier)

Length:	855 feet (261 m)
Displacement:	38,813 tons
Maximum Speed:	31 knots (36 mph/57 kph)
Range:	11,508 miles (18,520 km)
Crew:	2,000

Notes: The *Kaga* was a Japanese battlecruiser converted to an aircraft carrier. It carried about 97 aircraft. It was one of the ships that attacked Pearl Harbor in 1941. It was sunk by U.S. planes in 1942.

Japan

USS *Yorktown* (aircraft carrier)

Length:	869 feet (265 m)
Displacement:	27,100 tons
Maximum Speed:	33 knots (38 mph/61 kph)
Range:	17,262 miles (27,780 km)
Crew:	3,448

Notes: The USS *Yorktown* was an *Essex*-class aircraft carrier. With a crew of more than 3,400, it was virtually a floating city. The *Yorktown* carried between 80–100 aircraft.

United States

PT Boat

Length:	78 feet (24 m)
Displacement:	43 tons
Maximum Speed:	41 knots (47 mph/76 kph)
Range:	598 miles (962 km)
Crew:	11

Notes: "Patrol Torpedo" (PT) boats were small, fast, and armed with torpedoes to attack larger warships. Future President John F. Kennedy commanded PT-109 in the Pacific Ocean campaign against Japan.

United States

AIRCRAFT

Never has a weapon had as much impact on warfare as the airplane. Reconnaissance from the air, "eyes in the sky," made planning easier and more accurate. Ground troops could be helped directly with "close air support." And supplies could be flown in quickly from halfway around the world.

What the military calls "strategic bombing" perhaps had the biggest effect. Long-range heavy bombers, such as British Lancasters and American B-17 Flying Fortresses, flew hundreds of miles to reach targets in Germany and Japan, destroying factories, oil refineries, and railways in an effort to cripple the enemy's industrial strength and hasten the end of the war.

During World War II, for the first time in history, civilians were purposely targeted to weaken and demoralize the other side. This tactic ranged from the Japanese bombings of China and the German blitz on London, to the Allied firebombing of German and Japanese cities. It ended with the terrible, final, punctuation of the war: the atomic bomb attacks on the Japanese cities of Hiroshima and Nagasaki. Airpower changed the face of warfare forever.

An American B-25 Mitchell prepares to take off. The B-25 was a twin-engine medium bomber. It saw action throughout World War II. It had a crew of five, a range of 1,150 miles (1,851 km), and carried a bomb payload of 2,998 pounds (1,360 kg).

Germany

Junkers JU 87 Stuka

Length & Wingspan:	38/46 feet (12/14 m)
Range:	530 miles (853 km)
Maximum Speed:	255 miles per hour (410 kph)
Service Ceiling:	24,300 feet (7,407 m)
Crew:	2

Notes: The Stuka became an early symbol of the German *blitzkrieg* ("lightning warfare). It was a dive bomber with a distinctive "scream" when attacking. It was outmatched by Allied planes later in the war.

Germany

Messerschmitt Bf 109

Length & Wingspan:	30/33 feet (9/10 m)
Range:	350 miles (563 km)
Maximum Speed:	425 miles per hour (684 kph)
Service Ceiling:	41,665 feet (12,699 m)
Crew:	1

Notes: The Bf 109 was the most common German military aircraft of the war. Many versions were produced. It could intercept enemy fighters, bomb ground targets, and act as a reconnaissance aircraft.

United States

P-51 Mustang

Length & Wingspan:	33/38 feet (10/12 m)
Range (with external tanks):	2,050 miles (3,299 km)
Maximum Speed:	437 miles per hour (703 kph)
Service Ceiling:	41,700 feet (12,710 m)
Crew:	1

Notes: The P-51 played an extremely important roll during World War II, protecting groups of long-range bombers. In addition to being a fighter aircraft, the Mustang also attacked ground targets.

United Kingdom

Supermarine Spitfire

Length & Wingspan:	30/37 feet (9/11 m)
Range:	1,135 miles (1,827 km)
Maximum Speed:	369 miles per hour (594 kph)
Service Ceiling:	37,085 feet (11,304 m)
Crew:	1

Notes: The legendary British Spitfire fighter aircraft was agile and could climb very quickly. During the Battle of Britain in 1940, Spitfires shot down many enemy planes, thwarting a German invasion.

Mitsubishi Zero

Length & Wingspan:	30/40 feet (9/12 m)
Range:	1,120 miles (1,802 km)
Maximum Speed:	348 miles per hour (560 kph)
Service Ceiling:	35,700 feet (10,881 m)
Crew:	1

Notes: The Zero was a Japanese fighter aircraft that ruled the skies over the Pacific Ocean during the first part of the war. It was fast and nimble. But its weak defenses proved its undoing in later years.

Japan

Ilyushin IL-2

Length & Wingspan:	28/34 feet (9/10 m)
Range:	475 miles (764 km)
Maximum Speed:	255 miles per hour (410 kph)
Service Ceiling:	15,085 feet (4,598 m)
Crew:	2

Notes: The Ilyushin IL-2 was the Soviet Union's most important combat plane of the war. More than 42,000 were produced. It was used mainly to attack armored vehicles and ground troops.

Soviet Union

Avro Lancaster

Length & Wingspan:	70/102 feet (21/31 m)
Range:	2,530 miles (4,072 km)
Maximum Speed:	278 miles per hour (447 kph)
Service Ceiling:	24,895 feet (7,588 m)
Crew:	7

Notes: The Lancaster was the United Kingdom's main heavy bomber. It flew many missions over Germany, especially at night. Lancasters were also used in "dambuster" raids against German dams.

United Kingdom

Douglas SBD Dauntless

Length & Wingspan:	34/42 feet (10/13 m)
Range:	775 miles (1,247 km)
Maximum Speed:	255 miles per hour (410 kph)
Service Ceiling:	25,600 feet (7,803 m)
Crew:	2

Notes: The Dauntless was an American dive bomber that could withstand a lot of damage. It played a critical role in the victory over Japanese forces in the Battle of the Coral Sea and the Battle of Midway.

United States

The FLYING FORTRESS
B-17

The American B-17 was a long-distance, four-engine bomber. Its nickname was the "Flying Fortress." It was first used successfully by the United States Army Air Forces (USAAF) in Europe in 1942.

B-17s were high-flying, long-range bombers that were more accurate than other Allied aircraft, such as British Lancaster bombers. Many B-17s used a secret device called the Norden bombsight. This was an early type of computer that let bombardiers know the best moment to release the plane's bombs.

From bases in England and Italy, Flying Fortresses dropped 705,479 tons (640,000 metric tons) of bombs over Germany and Nazi-controlled territory. This was more than any other type of aircraft in World War II.

A precision bombing attack by American B-17 bombers against a German Focke-Wulf aircraft factory in Marienburg, Poland, on October 9, 1943.

The B-17 Flying Fortress was used mainly during daylight raids against industrial and military targets. The crew usually included two pilots, a bombardier, a radio operator, and five gunners. The Flying Fortress was legendary for its ability to absorb heavy damage, carry out its mission, and return to home base.

B-17G Flying Fortress

Length & Wingspan:	76/105 feet (23/32 m)
Range, with bombs:	1,095 miles (1,762 km)
Maximum Speed:	300 miles per hour (483 kph)
Service Ceiling:	39,700 feet (12,101 m)
Crew:	8–10

THE ATOMIC BOMB

The single most destructive weapon of World War II was the atomic bomb. American and German scientists raced to harness nuclear fission, the power created by splitting atoms. The American effort was called the Manhattan Project.

Germany surrendered before it could build an atomic bomb, but the United States successfully tested one on July 16, 1945. President Harry Truman decided to attack Japan with the new weapon in an attempt to bring the war to a swift end.

On August 6, 1945, a single B-29 bomber, the *Enola Gay*, dropped an atomic bomb on the Japanese city of Hiroshima. It exploded with the force of about 15,000 tons of TNT, destroying most of the city. Estimates vary, but approximately 70,000 to 80,000 people were killed.

On August 9, the city of Nagasaki was attacked, killing at least another 40,000 people.

The Japanese war effort was hopeless. On August 15, 1945, Emperor Hirohito announced Japan's unconditional surrender.

Facing page: A mushroom cloud from an atomic bomb blast rises over the city of Nagasaki, Japan, on August 9, 1945. *This page:* The devastated remains of Hiroshima, Japan, after the atomic bomb attack on August 6, 1945.

GLOSSARY

ALLIES

The Allies were the many nations that were allied, or joined, in the fight against Germany, Italy, and Japan in World War II. The most powerful nations among the Allies included the United States, Great Britain, the Soviet Union, France, China, Canada, and Australia.

AUTOMATIC WEAPON

A type of firearm that uses the force of the explosion of a shell to eject the empty cartridge case, put the next shell in position, and then fire it. This sequence continues as long as the trigger is pressed. A semi-automatic weapon fires once each time the trigger is pulled.

AXIS

The Axis powers were the World War II alliance of Germany, Italy, and Japan.

BLITZKRIEG

A German word meaning "lightning warfare." It described a new strategy that the German military used in World War II. *Blitzkrieg* called for very large invasions to overwhelm the enemy quickly with combined land and air attacks in order to avoid long, drawn-out battles.

DISPLACEMENT

Displacement is a way of measuring a ship's mass, or size. It equals the weight of the water a ship displaces, or occupies, while floating. Think of a bathtub filled to the rim with water. A toy boat placed in the tub would cause water to spill over the sides. The weight of that water equals the weight of the boat. Displacement is usually measured in long tons (one long ton equals 2,240 pounds (1,016 kg)). A long ton is slightly more than a normal U.S. ton, which equals 2,000 pounds (907 kg).

Fighter

A small, fast plane that is used to battle other planes in the air. Fighters were often used to escort large and slow bomber planes over enemy territory.

Great War

A nickname for World War I.

Heavy Bomber

A bomber capable of carrying large numbers of bombs great distances.

Howitzer

A short cannon that delivers its explosive shell in a high arc. Howitzers are useful for lobbing bombs when the enemy is relatively close, such as in trenches or over hilly terrain.

Nazi

The Nazi Party was the political party in Germany that supported Adolf Hitler. After 1934 it was the only political party allowed in Germany. This is when Hitler became a dictator and ruled Germany with total power.

U-Boat

An abbreviation of the German word for submarine, *unterseeboot*, which means "undersea boat."

INDEX